# WOMAN
## by the
# SHORE
### and other poems

*To my fellow bird-enthusiast*
*Peggy Lawson*
*with fond regards.*
*Bob Nero*
*October 30 / 91*

J.A.CARGON
1988
©

FOR LOUISE DE KIRILINE LAWRENCE

All royalties from this book are being donated to the
Louise de Kiriline Lawrence Nature Writers Award fund.
This award is being established to encourage
excellence in nature writing.

# WOMAN
## by the
# SHORE

### and other poems

*a tribute to*
*Louise de Kiriline Lawrence*
*by Robert W. Nero*

*Natural Heritage Books /*
*The Collector's Choice*

*Toronto*

**Canadian Cataloguing in Publication Data**

Nero, Robert W., 1922–
  Woman by the shore and other poems

ISBN 0-920474-59-4

1. Nature – Poetry.  I. Lawrence, Louise de
Kiriline, 1894–  .  II. Carson, Jim.   III. Title.

PS8577.E76W6 1990    C811'.54    C90-093638-X
PR9199.3.N47W6  1990

The publisher gratefully acknowledges the support of
the Ontario Arts Council.

Illustrations: James A. Carson
Design: Steve Eby

Printed and bound in Canada by Imprimerie Gagné Ltée

"our last yellow poppy
glows in the afternoon light
a beacon for a bumblebee...."

from *Last Bee, Last Flower*
by ROBERT W. NERO


"Even in the late 20th century,
or especially?, we need to be
made to feel the weight of
that bee and to see its echo
in the bobbing stem."

CANDACE SAVAGE, author,
Wolves
Eagles of North America
The Wonder of Canadian Birds

# CONTENTS

Introduction                          ix
Foreword                              xi

Woman by the Shore              3
First Snow                             4
Large Owl                              5
Wild Plum Tree                       6
Racing the Sun                       9
Weather Break                       10
Feather on My Sill                   11
Another View                         12
Lost Cause                            13
February Leaf                         14
First Outing                          16
Bog                                      17
April Twilight                         18
Unexpected Blessing              19
Ruby-Crown                          20
Robin's Nest                          21
May Day                               22
In a Wren's Eye                      23

| | |
|---|---|
| Visitors | 24 |
| Aspen Down | 26 |
| Quiet Sunday | 27 |
| Morning View | 28 |
| Late for Supper | 29 |
| Ruth in Flax | 30 |
| First Encounter | 31 |
| Two in the Sky | 32 |
| Unmowed Lawn | 33 |
| No Alarm | 34 |
| Ladybug, Ladybug | 35 |
| Fallen Feathers | 36 |
| Apprehension | 38 |
| Awakening | 38 |
| Migrant Juncos | 39 |
| Fall Robins | 39 |
| Fall Event | 41 |
| Salute | 42 |
| Last Bee, Last Flower | 43 |
| Late Fox Sparrow | 44 |
| Homeward Bound | 45 |
| This October | 46 |
| Sleepless Night | 48 |
| Teacher | 49 |
| *Author's Biographical Notes* | *51* |

# INTRODUCTION

Poetry, like music, is a universal language that is fresh with new meaning whenever it is read or heard. In this collection of poems, a seasoned naturalist reveals his thoughts as he pauses at unexpected moments, frequently in his backyard, and reflects on the meaning of what he has just observed or experienced. These are his own interpretations, often emotional, but so real that readers through their own thoughts can easily identify with the author. Although Dr. Nero had not planned to be a poet, he has successfully put his respect for nature into inspired verse. I am pleased that Bob has decided to share his poetry and I hope that this book will encourage him to write many more poems. In my opinion, this rookie poet has "earned his wings."

DR. MERLIN W. SHOESMITH
Chief, Biological Services
Manitoba Wildlife Branch

LOUISE DE KIRILINE LAWRENCE

Photograph courtesy Pat McGrath

# FOREWORD

The poem "Woman by the Shore" was sent to Louise de Kiriline Lawrence in April 1984 in response to a pensive letter I received from her after she turned ninety. When Barry Penhale asked me later if he could publish it along with his reprinting of MAR, Louise's story of a sapsucker, I was greatly flattered. It is not often that one has a chance to be so closely associated with someone one deeply admires. As I have said before, no one writes with greater clarity or better understanding of the lives of wild birds than Louise Lawrence.

In October 1989, Barry convinced me that publication of a small book of some nature poems I have written would make a nice tribute to Louise on her ninety-sixth birthday. So I really owe this honour to this grand, dear lady.

Margaret Belcher, a friend of mine in Saskatchewan, advised me that "there are only two subjects for lyric poetry — nature and love. And love poetry is so often self-conscious, and risks being trivial! Nature is never trivial." Although the poems in this book are largely nature-oriented, they still run the risk of being labelled trivial, and some of them, including "Woman by the Shore", *are* love poems. All except four were written in the past four years. Most were based on a fairly spontaneous reaction to an observed event. As an acquaintance once said, "Your poems are testaments to a sliver of time."

For encouragement in writing poetry I am indebted to more people than I can list. Special recognition goes to my wife, Ruth F. Nero, whose loving care has made my life so complete. In addition I need to thank Elizabeth Morton for critical review

of several pieces, some of which have appeared in *Trail &*
*Landscape*. This book would not have come into being except
for the insistence and support of Jane and Barry Penhale.

ROBERT W. NERO

Winnipeg, January 1990

# Woman by the Shore

There is a woman
I know, at Pimisi Bay
who says she's getting old
whose brave words
make me cry
when I thought I was through
with crying:
"I have reached
the all but obscene
age of 90…said in the sense,
that to reach for the exaggerated,
is to challenge the rational."

Little wonder that there are
tears on my face;
Louise speaks with clarion voice
and utter sensibility
for all of us.

I see her now
on a bench beside the bay
bird calls drawing her
out of herself,
words streaming through
her serene mind
a desire to write
making her blue eyes shine.

Listen to the loon
dear lady, let the voice of
the white-throat
send you my love.

# First Snow

The morning after our
first snow I found
the furrowed trails of
a shrew in our woods
a morning poem
a kind of knitting
darting here and there
half under, half above
an inch of fresh snow
with the same smooth rapidity
of my wife's needles
our shrew running through
soft snow as if it weren't there
slipping over the warp of
tree roots and fallen branches
its impetuous meanderings
inspired, excited by
the sudden cover of snow
a welcome relief from
bare November ground.

# Large Owl

"The bird is not as big as
it looks" say those who measure
with a finger
poked through feathers to body.

What nonsense! The owl is entire
of itself, massive in a coat of
soft plumes, and the perfect outline
of its round head is what the bird is,
no more, no less.

Each feather's tip is sensitive
to touch, a part of the bird
as leaves are part of a tree,
transient as molted feathers.
Twigs, buds and hidden roots
make a tree; the maple with its
distinctive shape, the symmetry of
a spruce…who would question
where the tree begins?

All those feathers can be moved,
compressed, fluffed out
expressing changing moods or
responding to weather.

True, its light feathers
are easily ruffled by
the wind, as a girl's hair,
another part of its charm.

If the size of a bird
is judged by its spirit
then this bird is even bigger
than it looks.

## Wild Plum Tree

This is confusing:
without snow on the ground
this mild December morning
seems like spring though
my footprints on the
crisp, frozen lawngrass
tell another story.

The absence of any fallen
leaves and the smooth, spaded
carefully raked black
garden plot attest to your
awareness of seasons;
and there stands the new
tree you watered until
the ground froze.

Not two months ago in
colourful autumn we went
in search of a
wild plum tree;
remember how we walked
together that warm evening
stepping quietly on new-fallen
leaves, leaving trees too big,
too strongly rooted or
too close to stumps.

I recall a sense of delight
in finding this tree
off by itself in a space
made familiar with our inspection,
grown gracefully beneath
bird calls and reaching for
the sun, higher than my head.

Some crimson leaves were
still attached, a sort of tag,
the price a moderate effort;
while I dug, you held the
thorny branches away
from my face
in tender complicity.

It took both of us to
free it from the forest floor
and cut the last hidden root,
but we took time to add
some of its own black soil
to our load.

It looked bigger in the back
of the car and still carried three
leaves — they were there even after
we had planted it.

Planting a tree one plans
the future, knowing from
experience how fast trees grow…
this was the right place, by itself
away from ash and oak.
In spring we'll see it from
the house and watch for it
to bloom before it leafs.

Wondrous, that from these
thin, crooked branches
held aloft today in silence
can emerge a billowy white veil
as often crowds the edge
of woods I've driven past and
wished I'd owned.

This will be our woods brought home;
when we go to test its fragrance
I'll rest my hand on your shoulder
and be glad.

# Racing the Sun

Riding a jet
out of the city
we raced the setting sun
red rim on the dark horizon
a mere bright curve against
dark, mantled clouds.

As we lifted to thirty thousand feet
the sun seemed to be rising
larger by the minute
until it was half-full!
bright, blazing orange-red
it hung suspended;
passengers ate peanuts, drank and
read magazines.

I watched that calm, raging
molten ball of fire
that sustains us all,
thrilled with a sense of
riding the sky
until at last it sank
out of sight
its voyage swift and sure.

# Weather Break

Shoveling fresh snow on a
late December morning
I stopped for an unexpected
bird sound, a slurred trill...
only chirping house sparrows
a "cluck" from our lone grackle
so what had I heard?
back to shoveling, then again
a squeaky, hesitant trill
our grackle with spread tail
essaying song!
having survived several chill
nights at forty below
he's feeling good for much
the same reason as me
this mild morning and blue sky
lifting our spirits.

# Feather on My Sill

It pleases me to see
a small gray feather
caught on the windowsill
fluttering in the breeze
some bird was here and
left a feather
for whatever reason...
some day, I think,
I could be in a
nursing home with
no window or one too
high for birds to visit
alone in a warm, dry room
dying of boredom
far from any bird feather.

# Another View

With snow on the ground
any walk reveals
patterns of plants
filagreed sinews
seed-heads, umbels
delicate inflorescences
tiny bouquets
we'd otherwise miss.

At thirty below
in an oak woods
the picture perfect
sprays of plants
above the snow
stop me in my tracks...
for that moment
I am warm.

# Lost Cause

Daily, our dog races
to a backyard shed
drops his chest to the ground
rump high, tail wagging
head thrust beneath the sill
hopefully searching for his friend —
a wary, shivering cottontail
that day after day crouched alert
while the dog scratched and
snuffled inches away —
alas, it's long gone
rudely savaged a month ago
by this overly friendly dog,
brought to the house
in bloody disarray
with the same exuberant interest
he now so jauntily displays.

# February Leaf

Late afternoon
on a calm winter day
after work
glad to be wandering along
a frozen trail over snowdrifts
in our treed backyard
relishing the still air
bright sunlight, squirrel tracks
and then discovered
a leaf still on a twig,
arrowwood, perhaps, judging by
the slender twig from which
it hung
just above the snow.
There were other leaves
in the woods
but this one held my attention:
golden-brown, curled
crisp, clean perfection...
it seemed to glow
in the warm light that bathed
aspen trunks and
lit the trail.

Is this old age
I wondered —
to stand and admire a dead leaf —
or am I finally learning
to see?

# First Outing

It seemed to me that we leaned upon the day
as much as upon each other;
I know that when I looked up
to follow the quiet flight of several robins
passing over us, I could have swooned,
caught up in their magic pull,
but for your arm firmly linked in mine.

Years, and illness, fell away at
the very moment I leaned my shoulder
into the dry brown grass
beside a crocus bloom
and watched your smile and tilted face
brightening to spring's own urge...
such delight could strike a fire
or break an unsure heart.

The shared intimacies of small birds
flitting through leafless boughs,
their short muted calls a proper cadence
for silvered aspen catkins and willow blooms
may bind us more than we know.

Oh, laughing girl, your throat builds
a measured rhythm that matches a host
of spring-maddened birds singing
in chorus, a soft sweet certainty
that winter lies behind us ... I have
your word that this is so.

# Bog

Cold nights
in April
when Northern Lights
lit up the sky

the startling reflection
of tamarack trees
in roadside pools.

# April Twilight

Our son gently adjusts binoculars
for his younger brother
reclining on spring's first lawn-chair,
peering up awkwardly to view
the early twilight moon.

Nearly black against the sky
a robin sits upright
sending its fluted whistle
in clear, measured phrases
to match another robin's song.

The boys turn their glasses
upon the heralding robin
perched in the crooked branches
of the catkin-drenched aspen
and offer imitative whistles.

The sky darkens, and in the deepening coolness
night sounds wash upon us.
The dog sits with ears alert, head aslant
while children's voices in the distance
rise, fall and cease,
and still the robin sings.

# Unexpected Blessing

Early morning routine
on a bright April day
driving automatically
radio fades in and out
of my mind
stop at a red light
then, a shivering "reee!"
— a Redwing's song —
half-heard, can it be?
I roll the window down
peer out, searching —
again that musical trill
there, atop a hydro pole
spunky Mr. Redwing
acting territorial on
a city street
this lord and master of
his marsh universe
lifting his wings and cape
blessing us all with song —
his voice recalls many springs…
I'm so entranced I miss seeing
the light change
shift awkwardly and pull away
smiling all the way
to the office.

# Ruby-Crown

This morning I
shared my breakfast
with a kinglet
it being spring
this feather of a bird
enjoying the same morning air
perilously small
flitting energetically
along a bough
beneath pendant
golden birch catkins
as I chomped my
fibrous cereal
it seized a tidbit
some insect egg or spider
almost at arm's length
and I recalled how
at a conference
many years ago
a young ornithologist
showed a film taken at
a kinglet's nest
at ninety-five feet
at the top of a great spruce
it took a tall tower
and a determined youth...
I thought how marvellous
are birds
and men.

# Robin's Nest

The young robins are growing
in their turquoise shells
turning slowly, evolving
repeating the pattern of
that chick embryo I studied
many years ago
and the patient parent
lies pressed upon the nest
bill open in this May heat
only a glinting eye
marks the coming and going
of our dog, people
door slams, car starts
while we count off days
to hatching and worry
about the squirrels...
the miracle is less the robins
nesting by our door
than how we stand together
after all these years
enjoying the simple bounty.

# May Day

The sight of fluffy aspen down
drifting like snow
against the green cedars,
covering my wife's garden,
sifting back and forth
betraying each small
erratic breeze
takes away my urge
to be serious...
it seems hopeless
I am caught up in
a wren's bubbling melody
I am turned to stone
by May sunlight
on our lawn
I am growing young
and silly.

# In a Wren's Eye

Wakened at dawn by
our wren's pulsing song
I follow his progress
as he moves from one side of
the house to another
pronouncing glory
throughout our yard.

Lured out by his enthusiasm
I stand shivering in the cool
morning, dew-drenched grass
soaking my shoes where a
sea of dew-drops sparkle
watching wren as he flits
along a practiced path
slipping through shrubs
in search of spiders
and dawn-numbed nymphs.

The wren's flight takes him
from darkest shade to brighter light
and I note he bears some green morsel
for his mate
where she lies secure
in the domed nest
drinking his liquid notes
from her warm bed of eggs.

Wrens are not concerned
about a dying tree that vexes me
or plans to move a fence
their vibrant lives move
at a carefully measured pace
led by militant genes
though they watch our neighbor's
gray cat where she stalks
through the garden
shaking wet feet.


## Visitors


Our children
wander through the yard
noting changes:
the size of trees
new flowers
a new birdhouse…
we behold them
with their children
heading into a future
we will not see;
our youngest son
chases an imaginary
soccer ball
with his infant son
on his shoulders,
we watch, smile and
lean against each other.

# Aspen Down

Aspen down lies wet
bejeweled at dawn
and in the cool mist
a robin
shuffles about on a nest
atop plump young.

Above the increasing hum
of busy motorists
speeding to work
in stacks and pools
of secretaries
I can hear
a meadowlark's shrill whistle
clear and sweet.

But come what may
let's stroll and dance
a little
now that summer's here
touch warm stones
and feel the grass...
write a poem
between us.

# Quiet Sunday

In the flower garden
stooped, slender figure of
my wife
tending her plants
she trowels them in
presses down the soil
with the same care
she crimps a pie-crust
hair drawn back, gleaming
gold, turquoise blouse
white-gloved hands.

I pause, blessed by
new awareness
taking in this
sunlit pageant on a
Sunday afternoon
and recall that as a
young girl
she transplanted wild
flowers before I knew her;
here she is still
writing next spring's sonnets
making music of a kind
with flowers.

So she tended the garden
of our children
those flowers of our life —
overwhelmed, I throw an
acorn at her
at its near fall she
looks up with feigned alarm —
for a long moment
we are very close.


## Morning View


Strands of spider silk
on my bedside window screen
split the morning sun asunder
making light dance
in rainbow hues
scintillating darts
that disappear with
earth's turning.
Now our maple's layered leaves
are golden-green and black against
the early sky —
before I lift my head I find
their pale blue shadows
dancing on the screen.

# Late for Supper

Downtown rush-hour traffic
hot, humid July evening
trying hard to be patient
as we nudge along
tapping my fingers
on the dashboard to
some jazz tune
to prove my nonchalance...
triumphantly let a bus
pull in front, savoring
the driver's quick wave...
finally emerge, slide into
an open lane with
a burst of speed
letting the car
draw me home
then, as I make my turn,
note with some surprise
that yesterday's uncertain
crushed carcass now shows
an identity tag
a backlit pinkish
rabbit's ear...
a satisfying sight,
the unknown, known.

# Ruth in Flax

She stoops to study
blue flowers in a flax field
gathering tiny blooms
to press for winter joy
while our excited spaniel
and I explore the road.

The dog dashes happily from
one intriguing scent to another
ignoring roadside litter
but I'm dismayed by
empty paint buckets and a mattress
holding down wild roses.

Turning back in disgust
suddenly I see my wife
as a figure in a painting
hair loosened by the wind
crouched in a shining blue field
white clouds on the horizon
reaching up to the sky.

When a distant bird sings
the tableau trembles
in a glad moment
this woman who finds beauty
in a roadside field
holds my heart.

# First Encounter

Walking awkwardly
on our freshly-cut lawn
in bright afternoon light
a hungry young grackle
begs in vain from
its glossy-plumed elders
hops towards sparrows
even boldly eyes a
feeding squirrel
but suddenly it stops
head drawn back
momentarily alarmed by
a backlit thistledown
blown its way by
a breath of air
an unexpected image
outside its evolutionary
program…
who could have guessed?

# Two in the Sky

On the bridge
in traffic
overhead there crossed
at the same time
these two:
a giant jet-plane
riding a vapour trail
a high-flying mallard
gliding on set wings
both arrow-shaped
precise mechanisms
that certain form of
their flying...the bird's
image more vivid.

The duck dropped down
to the river
the jet disappeared
and I moved on.

# Unmowed Lawn

In our backyard
the unmowed grass
lies heavy and sweet
rain-lashed
a green plain
with small lakes of
white clover
blossoming when it can
between one cutting
and the next
an epitaph to
my wife's absence.

When she returns
a week later
I note her dismay
at the unruly
creep of wilderness
in our yard
one wants it trim
and even, the other
likes to see it
catch the wind;
she thinks of her youth
playing croquet
on a level lawn, but I

remember fields
with meadow mice.

Later I slyly enjoy the
springiness and
sweet scent of her
new-mown grass...
the grass doesn't care
how we feel
it awaits our moods
laughing when we run
a silly race
and collapse in
each other's arms.

## No Alarm

A wasp hovers
so close
the breeze of its wings
alerts the hairs
on my arm.

# Ladybug, Ladybug

Astonished
that I should stop
and hold my breath
on seeing a ladybug
getting ready to fly
from the end of a twig,
lifting its orange hulls
unfurling its wings:
transparent gauze sheets
folded and stowed away
like any parachute,
on such unlikely material
this tiny Icarus goes off
in the bright sunlight
flying away home,
my luck to see it all.

# Fallen Feathers

Always, in late summer,
the feathers from molting birds
surprise me
crisp tokens
some as gay as flowers
decorating our lawn...
this narrow gray one
turned over is blue
and black and white
a primary from a jay
and here a golden feather
from a flicker
catches the late sun.
In fresh morning light
a grackle's feather
caught on a spruce bough
black on pale green
is as dramatic
as a living bird
enough to make me
catch my breath
though I like best the one
that fluttered down
as a grackle passed.

These plumes are proof
that autumn lies ahead...
I'll send them to my love.

# Apprehension

A wasp-like hum
close to my ear
a bump against my cheek —
as I gingerly
raise my hand
something goes down
my sleeve
interrupting my dozing
in the autumn sun;
careful inspection reveals
a friendly intruder
a black and orange ladybug
seeking winter shelter
with its own kind.

# Awakening

In the midst of
dawn thunder
and lightning-flashed rain
a blue jay's shrill cries
are pure brazen effrontery
a welcome refrain.

## Migrant Juncos

Smooth, gray feathers
conceal a crystalline skull
soft brain tissue
bears an imprint of
night-sky constellations
written in finest pen.

## Fall Robins

Robins in fall
ascend leafless boughs
with slow, fluttering flight
move hesitantly
across our lawn;
none of that
brightly-coloured, bold
hopping and stopping
in search of worms, gone
the bright, pealing songtime.

Their subdued colours
suit their mood and match
the fallen leaves;
they hop lightly to
our shallow pool
demurely taking turns
bathing quietly, more slowly
than robins should.

Their new white eye-rings
seem a kind of customs stamp
to speed them across borders
as they journey
down the continent.

In each fall
when robins leave
the land is still —
their going measures out
the year and marks
earth's turning...
their return is as certain
as the stars.

# Fall Event

Some years our ash tree
sheds its golden leaves
all at once
in a swirl of
wind and rain
but on this crisp, calm
blue overhead day
they loosen one by one
a slow trickling fall
until
by evening light
with bare limbs aloft
her yellow dress
lies at her feet.

# Salute

A late September day
warm, sunny, sparrows chirping
but here's my wife
dismantling her gardens
removing stakes, digging
pulling down vines
tossing faded flowers
on the mulch-pile.
"It's too soon" I pleaded
"Let's not spend this day on chores,
there's lots of time ahead,
come loaf with me in the sun."
"A lot you know" she said,
"I'd rather do it now than
when it's cold."
Next morning we found the lawn
white with frost, brittle
the birdbath frozen
the last of the garden plants
with velvet withered leaves
all black and brown
from the night's chill.
It takes a mother
someone who's nurtured five young
from infancy to adulthood
to read the signs of passing seasons
and remember birthdays...
no ecologist pays closer heed
to what lies ahead
or where we've been.

# Last Bee, Last Flower

Upright, motionless
in the still autumn air
our lone yellow poppy
glows in afternoon light
a beacon for a bumblebee
seeking one last meal
before its long sleep;
the bee's weight
brings the flower down,
its slender stem
bends as a bow
then rebounds
as the bee leaves;
a curious sight
yellow poppy nodding
as in a breeze.

# Late Fox Sparrow

It hopped into our
shallow garden pool
and stood still
the reflected image of
trees and sky
dancing at its feet —
feeling safe
it dipped and drank
then dropping all pretense
it bathed:
a shower of silver drops
lit the shadowed pool
wet the moss-furred rocks
as this symphony of
rusty-brown and grey
thrashed its fine feathers
rolled cold water off its
silken back
and emerged sparkling dry
a surprising feat
liquid only in
its gleaming eyes.

# Homeward Bound

Afterwork traffic
jostling for position
six lanes threading
into three,
attentive to cars ahead
behind and beside
classical music half heard
routine, mechanical
tomato can on a
conveyor belt
everyday.

On top of the bridge
stopped, bumper to
bumper
glanced aside
yellow October sun low
bright in my eyes
saw the river pale brown
rippled shiny fudge
and — surprise! — on
the railing
two wire-sharp illuminated
spiderwebs
photolike detail,
drove on
wondering if anyone else
noticed.

# This October

October was quiet, gentle
we worked in the garden
sifted mulch, delighting
in the treasure of
decomposed leaves
even as we raked up more,
sighing when a gust of wind
brought down another sackful,
again and again, until the
grass grew shiny with raking;
I watched you bending to
a flower bed, arranging for
spring, a crimson leaf caught in
your blond hair like a clasp.

October was golden
laden with fine scents
no chemist could repeat,
the fallen leaves, your hair
when I leaned close to exclaim
on the flight of a blue jay
gliding to a feeder
a blue silk banner unrolling
closing on itself on landing
scattering sparrows.

October was our calico cat
curled up, black chin on
white paws, tail wrapped
around, glittering eyes on
the scratching fox sparrows
silent, coiled spring
in the sun beneath a spruce.

# Sleepless Night

Cold electric ecstasy of
Northern Lights writhing foggily
across the sky
Orion perched high overhead
on a sleepless night
in late October.
Four in the morning is nothing
to this tame owl who
watches me with amusement
quietly staring down
at me when I murmur greetings
a low, soft hum, her call
and she lets me touch her
anywhere I please
her calm, composed demeanor
at this hour reminding me that
she's a night bird, sits
watching the sky move
interpreting cosmic creaks
rustles on the ground
faint sounds as a sudden breeze
lifts a bough; her gentle
acceptance of the night, of me
a quiet balm.

# Teacher

It takes a tame owl
to show me things
I'd otherwise miss
or overlook
or lose the importance of
such as
dead, dry aspen leaves
still on their twigs
rustling in a cold breeze
set to tapping against
each other —
a small thing
but it caught the owl's
attention for a moment
her head tipped up
motionless, watchful, listening
a delicate fall sound
I'd heard before
but never perceived.

# AUTHOR'S BIOGRAPHICAL NOTES

*E*ducator, ornithologist, writer, naturalist, Robert W. Nero studied at the University of Wisconsin under such eminent people as Joseph J. Hickey, John T. Emlen, Jr. and Aldo Leopold. He has lived and worked in Canada since 1955 and for the past 18 years has been with the Manitoba Department of Natural Resources, working mainly on rare and endangered species. Although he has many technical publications to his credit, Dr. Nero is equally well-known for his popular nature writings. His much-acclaimed book on the Great Gray Owl (lavishly illustrated by his close friend Robert R. Taylor), as pointed out in a review by Katherine McKeever, contains some writing "so lyrical it is almost poetry." In recent years, Nero has kept a tame Great Gray Owl for research and educational purposes. This bird, which has been exhibited in schools and at public functions for the past five years, is the subject of three of the poems in this book, one of which closes this volume.

Other books by Robert Nero include two Smithsonian Nature Books: *Redwings* and *The Great Gray Owl, Phantom of the Northern Forest*; *Manitoba's Big Cat*, a detailed account of the cougar (with R.E. Wrigley), was published by the Manitoba Museum of Man & Nature.

Winnipeg artist **James A. Carson** works for the Manitoba Department of Natural Resources. The sketches in this book were made available through the courtesy of the artist and the Department. Jim Carson's lively drawings also illustrate Robert Nero's *Redwings* published by the Smithsonian Institution Press.